MW00917836

ONE-MAN AIR FORCE
CAPTAIN DON S. GENTILE

AS TOLD TO IRA WOLFERT

First published by L. B. Fischer Publishing Corp. in 1944.

Copyright © Don S. Gentile.

This edition published in 2017.

TABLE OF CONTENTS

EDITOR'S PREFACE

Captain Don Salvatore Gentile, a Piqua, Ohio, boy, twenty-three, the only son of parents who emigrated to the United States from Italy, has been called by General Dwight D. Eisenhower "a one-man air force." Coming from the Commander-in-chief of the Allied forces, this is something a boy can put on his chest and strut behind for the rest of his life.

When the general said this to his face, Don blushed and looked as embarrassed as his military posture would permit. This boy who has destroyed thirty German airplanes — more than any other American has done in two wars so far, and the equivalent nearly of two whole Luftwaffe squadrons — is called "Gentle" by his mates at the Eighth Air Force Fighter Base in England. He is soft-spoken and self-effacing, a rather naive and quite unworldly boy, who has never done anything much or cared to do anything except fly. I moved in with him sometime in April about two weeks before he got his thirtieth plane. In those two weeks he lived a tragic, harrowing, prodigiously dangerous climax to his life. It was the peak few men ever attain and even fewer, once attaining, survive.

At such a time one can get to know a man very well, and this, I think, I managed with "Gentle" We spent our evenings and nights in beds separated by a radio whose soft music he turned on to soothe the banging his beaten-up nerves take. He spent his days among the enemy's bullets, sometimes killing the enemy and sometimes seeing the enemy kill his friends.

Then he returned to the sheets and the mattress and the windows that faced the night of a quiet English countryside and the radio that softly brought music from home. The music led him on, and the quiet of the night outside and the terrible excitements of the day and the thoughts of what awaited him next day or surely the day after — they all led him to talk more, he told me, than he had talked in all his twenty-three previous years.

He talked about his life to me, and I have tried to set it down within the limits of space as truly as I could, for it seemed to me an important life for the rest of us to understand.

For this is not only the story of "a one-man air force" against the Huns; nor is it only a story of the fluctuations, failures and successes of our air war against the Luftwaffe. It is also the story of a new type of American — one who has been growing up all around this older generation of ours, sometimes, it seems, while we were hardly looking and who will be ready to take over and make use of the air power that is predicted now to lie just beyond the war.

"Gentle" is one of them, one of the best examples of the type, I think — a boy who is shy, self-effacing and rather unsure when he stands on the ground, but who comes into his magnificent own when he becomes air-borne.

Ira Wolfert

CHAPTER 1

The theory of fight between fighter planes is very simple. You see the enemy, grab for his coattails, hold on to them, put your guns up against his back pocket and press the trigger. But while you are reaching for his coattails, he is reaching for yours. You make your grab and he twirls out of the way and into position to make his grab. Whereupon you twirl with a twist that will put you in a fair way to grab him and so on and so on, grab-twirl-twist, grab-twirl-twist, sometimes for quite a long time — for ten minutes or maybe fifteen minutes — until at last somebody has grabbed hold for good and the other fellow starts to die.

That's the dogfight. It is rather a rare occurrence in modern war. I don't suppose I had more than six or seven of them in all the times in the last two years that I have mingled with the Huns.

For the most part, the work is something like that of a football team. We fly formations where each man is counted on to be able either to carry the ball for a touchdown or to run interference for the man doing it. The idea is to put protection around the coattails, and usually we fly with the more experienced man in the number one position and the less experienced man in the number two spot, which is close on number one's wing and slightly to the rear.

Number one makes the play if the enemy is ahead of us, but if he bounces us or is first spied astern of us then the formation wheels around and number two man will be in the number one spot making the play while the others fall in behind to guard his and each other's coattails.

The point is that the man in the best position to go across the goal line when the goal line is sighted is the fellow who usually carries the ball while the others run interference for him. That's the routine order of the day-to-day business. Individual scores depend in the same way as in a football game, upon how hot the whole team is. It's hard to be cold when the team is hot. But the dogfight, in which your plane is against another, or two or six others, is not day-to-day routine. It's a big deal in our business.

The whole thing goes in a series of whooshes. There is no time to think. If you take time to think you will not have time to act. There are a number of things your mind is doing while you are fighting — seeing, measuring, guessing, remembering, adding up this and that and worrying about one thing and another and taking this into account and that into account and rejecting this notion and accepting that notion. But it doesn't feel like thinking.

After the fight is over you can look back on all the things you did and didn't do and see the reason behind each move. But while the fight is on, your mind feels empty and feels as if the flesh of it is sitting in your head, bunched up like muscle and quivering there.

When I shot three Huns out of the air, half my guns jammed at the start, and so the most I could have been shooting during the whole mission, including test firing, was a little more than ten seconds. How long those seconds seemed!

Now, when you've got a good hold on the enemy's tail and are clobbering him well, it seems then he never will die. Each part of a second then doesn't feel like time at all, but is so slow, so very slow and so endless. Armor-piercing incendiaries hit him all over. They cloud him up all over and go all over him like snake tongues. That's what they look like — little red snake tongues, hundreds of them, licking at him, flicking him poisonously all over. That goes on and on, each little flick quick as a twist, but the whole thing so slow, so endless.

Then black smoke starts out of him and goes slowly and endlessly out of him and glycol, too, is seeping out of him. At first it comes as if you've squeezed it out of him and then a cloud of it appears. Glycol is the fluid that keeps the motor from overheating. You can't fly more than a minute or so without it. It comes out into the air looking white, and when you see it coming out well, in a pour, then that's the end. That is the wind of death blowing up to storm proportions in him, blowing his life's blood out of the holes you've made in him. It's a small pour at first, usually thin, like a frosty breath; then bigger, bigger, bigger and always slow and endless and stuck into your eyes and stopped there like a movie held still.

And after that, sometimes when you're really clobbering him and are really all over him, hammering his guts out, pieces start coming off him. It's nuts-and-bolts stuff at first, then bigger things, big, ripped-off looking things as if you're tearing arms and legs off him and arms and legs and the head of him are going slowly and endlessly over your shoulder.

When you look back at it or see it from the outside, it just seems like one whoosh and, bang! the Hun is dead. But not when you're in it. Oh, no, not then.

And when the enemy has got you and is clobbering you, that's slow, too. It's like lighted matches being dragged slowly across the bunched-up flesh of your brain. It feels like your brain is dissolving away under the pain on top of it. It's a fight to keep your brain together, and while you're fighting this fight, putting, it seems, your two hands on your mind holding it in one piece with all the strength in your fingers, how long it seems to last and how far away the end you want seems to be.

I've had help in fighting this kind of fight from two Huns with whom I struck up a brief acquaintance on separate occasions. Each fought very well. They were crafty and had courage. One of them I thought was going to be real, serious trouble to me. The other I thought was going to be able to get away to fight another day.

But suddenly, I don't know, something happened in their minds. You could see it plainly. Their brains had dissolved away under the pressure of fear and had become just dishwater in their heads. They froze to their sticks and straightened out and ran right into their graves like men stricken blind who run, screaming, off a cliff.

Since then, whenever a Hun has gotten my tail into his teeth, I've thought of those two fellows. Ordinarily, the Hun appears to you, with his oxygen mask on and no life or movement in him, as not a man at all, but just a gadget in that machine of his. Those two fellows were the only Huns I ever thought of as people, and it helped me a lot to do so. It kept me several times from doing what they had done — from going blind and running, screaming, off a cliff.

CHAPTER 2

Gentile told me the air war really started when the Mustangs came.

At that time the important thing to me about my score against the Germans, and I think the thing that makes it worth a person's reading time, is that it symbolizes the whole course of the air war to date and is, in its small way, the chart of it.

I started flying in Spitfires. June 22, 1942 — nearly two years ago now — was the day I put myself up against the Huns for the first time. The Spitfire of that day was a defensive weapon, which could not carry the war far into enemy territory. It could just about go into his front-line trenches.

Later, the group I was attached to got Thunderbolts. At that time the Thunderbolt was a plane for limited offensive fighting. It could beat the Luftwaffe out of the neighborhood of our home, but could not follow him all the way back and pull down his own house over his ears.

Finally, we started flying Mustangs. This was the plane for unlimited offensive action. It could go in the front door of the enemy's home and blow down the back door and beat up all the furniture in between.

Our side was still on the defensive. We had to do more running away than running after. It was not until August 19, 1942, that I got my first German planes, a Junkers 88 and a Focke-Wulf 190. That was over Dieppe, at the time of the great raid on that port-the time, if you remember, when our side was turned loose on the offensive, if only for a day.

Through all the long months that followed, while the Eighth Air Force was building itself up from the ground, we prepared to take the offensive away from the Germans, and then with the Thunderbolts really started to go out and get it.

The big bombers were the heavy guns in this phase of the war. Their job was to beat the German air force out of Western Europe, and our job was to help keep the German air force from stopping them.

In those days we flew close support for the bombers. When the German fighters came in on the bombers — not before — we turned into fighters and shot at them. As soon as an individual plane or a single formation broke off to attack, we hustled back to the bombers. The thing was, it was a limited offensive. We couldn't go all out. We had to peck and peck at them until they were weak enough to be trampled down.

In those days I got some "probables" and some "damages." We could not follow the enemy fighters past the point at which they broke off the attack. We had to climb back to the bombers to make sure they were not hit from another side. So we could not follow the "smokers" or the partially clobbered to see them crash or, if more shooting was needed, to do that and finish them off.

The score of the whole group was low in those days and it stayed low. It was April 2, 1943, when the group quit Spitfires for Thunderbolts, and about June or July of that year when we started noticing a kind of faltering in the Luftwaffe. The pecking of the bombers and ourselves was beginning to take effect. It looked as if the time would soon come when we'd be turned loose to trample them down.

But the German is a crafty foe and he began then one of those "planned retreats" of his. He took many of his planes out of France, Holland and Belgium, and there we were sitting in our Thunderbolts, unable to follow after them.

The Fortresses and Liberators barreled right into Germany after the Luftwaffe. We could go along with them only so far and no further. The bombers had to go the rest of the way without us. The Luftwaffe just waited for the bombers to go past our sphere of action. Then they hit and didn't stop hitting until our bombers were back with us. Then the Luftwaffe strutted back home like dogs which chase a marauder out of the front yard and are content to let it go at that.

Meanwhile, the home front was busy on the Mustang. With the Mustang there was no place for the Luftwaffe to retreat. That plane put the Huns' back right up against the wall, but we did not have enough fighter cover in the latter part of last year, and the early part of this year, to give anything but close support to our bombers. Fighter planes had to fly close formation to protect one another and had to devote themselves to breaking off enemy attacks, but could not follow through on the Hun making his getaway.

This was the old pecking days all over again — pecking, pecking and pecking at the enemy's strength until he was weak enough to be trampled down. But this time there was this important difference: when we would get strong enough to start trampling he would have no place to run. He would have to stand and fight.

The time finally came for us in late February of this year. There was no more need to put all our planes in the close support of the bombers. There was no more need to keep the formation at any cost. We were sent out there to go and get and clobber the Nazis. If they wouldn't come up into the air we would go down against their ground guns and shoot them up on the ground. Get them, that was the idea; kill them, trample them down.

It was this time I, personally, was ready for. I had been waiting to fly, and flying was practically my whole life. In the two years of mixing it with the Germans I had learned a great many things that you can't learn in any but the hard way. And there were many in Colonel Don Blakeslee's group who were in the same condition. It was no accident that when the bell finally rang for the big fight Colonel Blakeslee's team became, in seven weeks of the happiest, craziest hayriding ever, the highest-scoring outfit in the whole league.

In all this time of the rising and falling of the tide for us, the Luftwaffe has deteriorated steadily, but it has been a thing about which I have been slow to make up my mind. The Nazis all seemed like champs to me at first, but as I started to learn my business I began to notice that some of them did not know their business as well as others. In recent days I have noticed more and more Huns who do not know their business. This may be because the older I get in this game the more critical I become and the easier it is for me to spot a boy who is green at the trade and worried and not sure of himself and on the defensive all the way.

But I don't think that's the whole reason. I think it is true that the Luftwaffe consists more and more of new boys as the old hands get killed off. However, there are still quite a lot of the old hands around, and they are real hot shots. They know two things you need to know in this business: how to kill and how to keep from being killed. There is nothing defeatist about their attitude — nothing that I can notice anyway.

So, by and large, I don't think this team I'm on would have run up the score it has if things hadn't broken just right for it — if the bell hadn't rung to go all out at exactly the time when it was ripe to do just that. I know that's true in my case.

I have a feeling now, looking back over the last few weeks, that all my life everything I have done in it has gone to fit me to take advantage of the weeks between February 20 and April 8.

CHAPTER 3

I can't remember the time when airplanes were not part of my life and can't remember ever wanting anything so much as to fly one. Once I had started I had to keep flying.

When I was six years old I started pestering my father, Patsy, into taking me down to Troy every Saturday and Sunday to see the Wacos outside the plant there. Then I used to go down by myself and when I was in my early teens I began nagging at Dad for flying lessons.

His eyebrows went way up when I first mentioned it, and my mother's mouth pulled way down. I remember how they looked. It was plain in their faces that what I had asked for seemed undreamt of to them and absolutely impossible. And to me it seemed impossible that it should be undreamt-of by anyone. It was a kind of shock to me. I think I felt then for the first time a person who is different from his parents and lives in a separate world.

Dad used every now and then to give me money to go out on dates. He was not a rich man. He had come to the United States at the age of fourteen and started to work as a water boy in the gas company at Columbus. He remained with them for twenty-five years. He rose to be foreman and he kept up our home and raised my sister Edith (who is two years younger than myself) and me on $50 and $60 a week, saving his money until, when repeal came, he could do what he liked, which was to open a bar and grill and live off of that.

But even though he was not rich, he is what they call "regular" and he was really wonderful to me. When he gave me $5 to take a girl out I'd put $3 or $4 into the bank and splurge the rest on the girl. When he gave me $10 I'd put $8 or $9 of it into the bank. Dad was amused and Mother was delighted, I think, but I knew what I was doing.

I wanted to fly.

I was pretty bashful and afraid of people, and Dad, who is a ground-minded man, chose his own way to correct that. When I was sixteen, in 1936, he had me come in to wait on tables in the good old Genova Bar and Grill. It worked out all right, I guess. Anyway, I got so that I could talk right along with the boys and kid them back as I brought them their beer.

But it was not until I was seventeen that I finally got into an airplane. At that time I felt I had come to the place where I belonged in the world. The air to me was what being on the ground was to other people. When I felt nervous it pulled me together. Things could get too much for me on the ground, they never got that way in the air. Flying came into my mind like fresh air smoked up into the lungs and was food in my hungry mouth and strength in my weak arms. I felt that way the first time I got into an airplane. I wasn't nervous when I first soloed. There was excitement in me, but it was the nice kind you get when you're going home after a long, long, unhappy time away.

Dad gave up then and started buying me a half hour's flying time every Sunday. It cost about $10, depending on the kind of plane you could rent.

Then I began pestering him to buy me an airplane. His eyebrows went up again and my mother's mouth went down again. They said no, no, no, and I said yes, yes, yes. I found a man with a homemade, single-seater, open-cockpit plane, which he was willing to sell for $300.

Mother said I was crazy and Dad said he wouldn't hear of any such thing. So I went down to the bank and drew out the $300 and paid it over.

Somebody, we never knew whom, called up Mother anonymously and said, "Your son bought himself a death trap to fly in." This made Mother rush screaming down to the airport to cancel the sale. It turned out that the man who had sold me the plane was a crook. He had somebody fly the thing off to Indiana at Mother's first scream and Dad went down with me to try to get my money back. We couldn't, without lawyers, and Dad figured it would be too expensive that way.

"Okay," he told me. "You've learned a lesson. You've got $300 worth of experience now."

But I brought up the subject again and again and another time and another time — every chance I could. Finally, Dad bought me a single-seater biplane Aerosport for $450. When Dad gives in, he gives in good.

The general reputation I had in Piqua was not, I think, too good. The folks around there thought I was a pretty crazy kid. I played football and baseball for Piqua Central High and managed to make the second team in basketball and was average in my studies, going along with the middle of the class. There wasn't anything they could pick on there.

But when I got into an automobile that had a lot of horses to gallop, I galloped them. I'd race every car on the road. I'd go 100 miles an hour sometimes when the cops chased me, because they were in Fords and could make eighty, while I had Dad's Lincoln Zephyr.

Maybe twists and turns and skids and looking back while driving wasn't good citizenship on the Ohio roads, but it turned out to be good training for driving over Germany.

On Saturday afternoons I would beat up the town in my airplane, and the cops chased me in that, too. I could see their cars running after me, trying to get my number. I'd raise the hair on everybody's head with my propeller. I'd blow in the curtains on Betty Levering's house and make the geraniums in Marge Dill's front yard give up their petals.

Then the cops would come into our parlor and Dad would give them cigars. "Was that you flying low?" they'd ask me.

"Did you see a number on the plane?" I'd say.

"Hell," they'd say. "You was going 900 miles a minute. Who could count the numbers?"

After a while they'd go off, saying, "You've got to quit this low flying around town. You know it ain't safe."

And it was against the law, but I did it. I did it because I wanted to. I wasn't showing off, although maybe there was some of that in it. Anyway, it didn't feel like showing off to me.

Driving fast, flying low, stunting, putting my brain and my power over a machine against death and telling death, "Catch me if you can" — that was the kind of competition I needed to make myself feel alive. Every man needs competition. If he's a scholar, it's how much can he learn; if he's got a job, it's how well can he do it; or if he's unhappy in it, it's how much can he get away with gold-bricking.

Getting the most out of a machine was my competition. I thought I knew what a machine could do and what I could do with a machine, and particularly when flying I never was nervous or afraid or felt in danger — even when I zipped a wingtip right under the nose of death.

The way it all worked out, it was all right. It was just what I needed for war. I remember September 1, 1939, well. The Piqua Daily Call came into the school and the teachers ran out of their classrooms and the kids, too, and everybody stood in the corridors reading the big, black headlines: "Hitler Invades Poland." A lot of fellows could read their death sentences in that headline. Millions and millions of fellows all over the world read their death sentences in that headline that morning.

But I didn't feel that way. I felt, standing in the school corridor there in Piqua with all that excitement all around me, that I was going to get into the war. But I was ready for it. I had confidence in myself if they would get me off the ground and put me into the air.

CHAPTER 4

My father and mother and I worked it out together. They wanted me to go to college, and I wanted to go to college and get ahead and make something of myself. But I told them this is the kind of fellow I am: it's airplanes or nothing for me. Anywhere else I'd be a round peg in a square hole for the rest of my life. Put me in an airplane and I know I am sure I can make something of myself.

Dad saw that. Mother did, too, I guess, although she wouldn't admit it. She never understood why anybody wanted to fly, and when it came to the flesh — her own flesh — she was more than puzzled. She was frightened. She was like a hen that had hatched out a strange bird.

I told them we were going to get into the war soon and that I'd be drafted. I'd never be allowed to finish college. I applied for admission to Ohio State, but that was just to make my folks happy while the argument went on. Without a college degree, I told them, I couldn't fly for the United States Army. When they drafted me, I said, it would be the infantry for me or tanks or something and I wouldn't have the chance to live that I'd have if I could fight in an airplane. Not me — not the type of person I was. But, I said to them, if I joined the R.A.F. now, I'd get to be a pilot, and when we came into the war I could transfer over and be a pilot in the U.S. Army Air Force, college degree or not.

France fell, and the Battle of Britain began, and I kept on fighting the Battle of Piqua, Ohio, to give myself a chance for life in the war that was coming down on all of us.

"You'll see," I told my Dad. "I'll make my mark in this war if I can fly in it." I used the name and story of Captain Eddie Rickenbacker on Dad to show him what a man could do, and finally I won the Battle of Piqua.

In September, 1940, in the same week I was supposed to go off to Ohio State, Dad drove me down to Cleveland to enlist in the R.A.F. In all the long drive he didn't say much; he just sat there looking like an unhappy little boy. Then when I got on an airliner to go off for training, Mother fainted at the airport. And a year later, after I had got my wings and came home for my last overseas leave, Mother wouldn't get off the train that was taking me away from her. She wept and clung to her seat, and they had to hold up the train until Dad finally led her off.

My sister Edith was very frank with me. She told me what a louse I was to do what I had done, and I felt like a louse as the train pulled me on past Ohio and toward Canada. There was a taste of sorrow in my mouth all the way, and sorrow lay in my eyes like clouds so that everything on the train and in the scenery there looked strange. But I knew that what I was doing was right. It was the only thing and the best thing for me to do.

When Dad said goodbye, he told me, "Son, you're on your own now. If you're in trouble just write to me and I'll help you. Whatever it is and wherever you are I'll help."

I have thought of that often since then. I have thought of it over Abbeville and Dieppe, over Berlin and a lot of other foreign places. I once sat all night all by myself in our squadron's quarters, where I was the only survivor out of the whole squadron, and thought of what Dad had said. But I always wrote him that everything was going fine.

Making a fighter pilot is a long business. My instructors had worked hard back home, and when I was graduated I was graded "better than average pilot." But flying an airplane is only a part of fighting with one, and most of the other part a man has to learn in actual combat. He has to learn from his fellow soldiers and from the enemy.

I was lucky enough to get attached to the Eagle Squadron, in which some of the finest fighter pilots who ever lived were working — lucky enough to get into the war at a time when a man could afford to be cautious about learning and could feel his way and not just have to throw himself against the enemy and try to clout him down blindly.

I learned a lot from the enemy, too. In the beginning we were up against Goering's Abbeville Kids — those yellow-nosed Focke-Wulf, veteran big-timers. There were not many better teachers of attack and defense than those killers, and of those who were better teachers quite a few were in the Eagle Squadron.

There are two things a fighter pilot must have to do his work in combat and that he can't really acquire anywhere else except in combat: confidence in his ability to kill and confidence in his ability to get away when in trouble.

If you feel you can kill and feel they can't kill you, then you'll have the offensive spirit. Without that offensive spirit — ability to lunge instantaneously and automatically like a fighting cock at the enemy the moment you spot him — you are lost. You either "go along for the ride," as we call it when a fellow hangs back and doesn't make kills, or eventually you get shot down.

I know, because it took me quite a long time to build up confidence in myself, which I had thought I had when I left home, and there was quite a long time when I went along just for the ride.

CHAPTER 5

When I first reached England early in 1942 there was some notion of putting me to work in the Royal Air Force as an instructor, but I took a Spitfire out one day and beat up a greyhound racetrack, where there was a race going on and the notion ended right there.

When I flew over the dog-track the dogs were tearing after the rabbit and the customers were cheering them on. But when I finished buzzing the track the dogs were running and yowling all over the park and the customers were sprinting after them. Some of the customers, I was told later, even overtook and passed the dogs. Only the mechanical rabbit continued, undaunted, on its way.

Harsh words were uttered at great length and a decision was quickly reached that I did not have the temperament suitable for an instructor.

And I didn't at the time. I wanted to fight.

On June 22 of that year, as I've said, I went "over the top" against the Germans for the first time. It was not easy or pleasant, nor did my conduct give me anything to be proud of. I concentrated on staying alive. We went against Boulogne. "They'll be there waiting for you," the control tower told us over the radio, "so be careful."

I have a habit when I am frightened of talking to myself silently — but the words are so plain in my head that it's almost as if they were echoing there with real sound. "Now, boy," I'd say to myself, or call myself "Squirt" or "Son," and tell myself to just take it easy and I'd be all right. But whatever I told myself that day I kept thinking, "Oh, Mama!"

We went along fast in a good, tight formation, like a bunch of killers going to town, I guess, but I kept sitting up there in the middle of the posse looking like one of the boys, no doubt, but thinking what a kid I was. I was twenty-one years old then, and what was I doing here, I asked myself, when where I wanted to be was at home in my mother's lap.

I was flying number two to Colby King that day. King had been a test pilot for Lockheed and was a veteran at shooting the Nazis down. "Just stay with me," King said, "until you get confidence. If you keep on my wing I'll take care of you."

That's all I thought of — to keep on his wing. The radio suddenly filled up with shouts: "Break! They're bouncing us! He's on your tail, P (for pectin). You damn fool! He's on your goddamn tail!"

But I didn't see anything except Colby King's wing and I stuck to it through turns, twists and dives, and it was not until I came home that I found out some of the Germans had been killed and some of our boys, too.

There wasn't anything there to give me confidence. I didn't feel like a veteran after that first show. But I suppose I must have learned something because on the second show when we tangled with Goering's famous Abbeville Kids in their yellow-nosed Focke-Wulfs, I at least saw them. I saw one of them go down and one of our Spitfires go down.

I kept gingering along like that, concentrating on holding on to Colby King's wing and staying alive, never daring to shoot my guns at a German until July 31 when, suddenly, Colby King got shot down right in front of me, and there I was all by myself in the middle of the Abbeville Kids with nobody to help me.

Four or five Huns had bounced us from the rear and six or seven of them from head-on. I rolled out and then saw that one of the Huns had rolled with me and picked me out as his piece of cake. I figured I couldn't shoot him down, as I didn't know enough about the business of fighting a plane yet to match his skill and experience. I figured, too, I didn't have skill enough even to evade his attack.

Well, if you can't win by matching your brain against another man's, then your only hope is to match your body against his. And that's what I did against this Jerry. I bet the body I had built up on Piqua (Ohio) Central High's athletic fields against the body he had built up goose-stepping for Hitler.

I went into a spiral dive at 30,000 feet, making turns tight enough to black myself out. I hoped to be able to stand it better than he. I kept the controls almost solid, so I'd black out and keep blacked out until I felt consciousness going and felt the strength draining soupily out of my muscles. Then I would release the stick until I could see dim, gray clouds. Then I would pull the stick back again fast, until the curtain of black dropped over my eyes and my consciousness began again to drain away sluggishly with a thick feeling — as when blood is draining out of a body wound.

Jerry couldn't take it. When I got down on deck I saw I had lost him and I ran straight for home like a whipped boy. But I was not entirely whipped. I had known from my first flight that I was playing in the big leagues — in a game that is very tough wherever it is played; the toughest, most reckless game, in fact, that any human being ever thought up to play. But after cheating that Hun of his piece of cake I began to get confidence that even if I couldn't make the pace in the game I at least had a chance to go along with it.

Less than three weeks after that I had enough confidence in myself not only to evade the Nazis but to go after them and kill them. That was over Dieppe on August 19, 1942, the day of the big raid there.

I saw a Junkers 88 going down to lay his eggs on what was temporarily our beach. He was diving, and I dove with him and under him so that he couldn't see me and I could get up speed. Then I pulled up behind him and let him have it. I didn't take any evasive action, I felt so confident. I was packed swollen with blissful ignorance and I just threw a barn door full of bullets at him. He jettisoned his bombs in the water trying to get away, and I banged him again and he burned on the beach. That crew was all dead inside, burning in that burning plane.

Right after that while I was still down on the deck crazy with confidence and a sense of power, I saw two yellow-nosed Focke-Wulfs under me — some Abbeville Kids looking for a fight to get into. I got onto their tails and shot down one, but the other got away from me.

That day gave me a happy feeling, and I had found out another thing about myself to give me confidence — the quality of my eyes. I had always known my eyes were better than most. I have 20/10 vision. Twenty-twenty is perfect, but 20/10 is better than perfect for a fighter pilot. I can read the bottom line on the eye chart and also the manufacturer's name.

On that day over Dieppe I found out just how useful it is to have better vision — that half-second or one-second advantage it gives you over your enemy in picking the black speck of him out of a scud in the sky or the fleckedup grays, blues or blinding, bleached-out yellow is the difference, other things being equal, between killing or being killed.

But I still was a long way away from being a hot shot. The Junkers 88 hadn't a chance, but I knew if those two Abbeville Kids had had their brains with them they could have got me easier than I could have got them. I had luck there, and a man in the fighter pilot business can't feel a trust in his luck until he feels he can roll his own luck when and as he needs it.

CHAPTER 6

Looking back now from my vantage point after some hundreds of scraps with the Germans — of bouncing them and of being bounced and of the bangs and prangs and clobberings and of being clobbered — I would say now that in those ancient days of 1942 and 1943 the confidence I had in my ability to kill the Nazis and to keep them from killing our men was misplaced.

I know now how much remained for me to learn before I could handle myself in the rough, fast, big-time company they have operating over Europe. But in those days I didn't even know how little I knew.

After I had a few fights under my belt and made a few scores I became again what I had been before the war — a kid full of beans, who, when he sits in an airplane, feels there is nothing in the world that can master him. Fortunately for me, our side of the war was up against a situation in those years that prevented me from acting on my belief in myself. Otherwise, I probably would have had my beans cooked in some gasoline fire long before I learned how much there is to know besides flying about this business of fighting.

We were on the defensive then. When we first started going on the offensive with Flying Fortresses and Liberators our fighter planes remained on the defensive, their job being to provide a close escort for the heavy artillery and not to mix it with the Germans but just to break off their attacks.

During most of this period Captain Carl (Spike) Miley, a Toledo, Ohio, boy whose savvy I have only now begun to appreciate, was my flight leader and he kept a tight check on me to hold me in the formation. I wanted to make the touchdowns. He wanted to keep the team together, running the interference for the touchdown-scoring bombers. We didn't quarrel, but I became restless under his control. And the more restless I got, the firmer did Spike pull the reins. When he finished his tour of operations last September and was ordered home, Spike recommended me for his place as flight commander. After I got the promotion he took me aside.

"All right," he said to me, "you're red hot and it's natural you should want to be a firecracker over here. But you've got boys following you now who have things to learn before they get red hot. They're going to follow you wherever you take them. Remember that when you take them anywhere. It's not only your brains that are going to get knocked out, but the brains of the kids who are depending on you."

That gave me a new slant, and I kept the boys under as tight a rein as Spike had kept me. But the whole thing did not fall into place for me until January 14 of this year when I bounced myself into the bag and I had to use every single thing I had ever learned in combat to get out with the Germans dead and myself alive.

There is a little song Lieut. Jack Raphael of Tacoma, Wash., worked up to commemorate the occasion. It goes to the tune of "Tramp, Tramp, Tramp, the Boys Are Marching." Here are the words:

"Help, help, help! I'm being clobbered
Down here by the railroad track.
Two 190's chase me around

And we're damn near to the ground,

Tell them I got two if I don't make it back."

The song is good, but the way the story really went was like this:

We were on a sweep in the Paris area, and down there somewhere I saw and reported a group of some fifteen or twenty Focke-Wulf 190's flying east about 5,000 feet below us. We bounced them, and I picked out two stragglers. I yelled to my number two man and he said: "Keep going; I'm with you!"

The Huns turned into me, and we closed the distance between us at better than 700 miles an hour. At the rate of 700 miles an hour you can eat up all the distance there is in one gulp, but while you're doing it it seems slow. You can think of a thousand things, and nothing seems to be happening in your life except that the plane is coming slowly toward you and you're living a lifetime — as if it was a speed-up movie reel — and aging fast and growing old and older and looking suddenly at the end of your life in just about the time it takes to say it.

This moment of closing in on a head-on attack can sometimes decide a whole battle. The question is: "Who will break off the attack first?" The one who turns away first goes on the defensive, and the fellow with the guts to stick it out swings on his tail and has a chance to make the kill.

So I just sat still in the cockpit, with my thumb on the gun teat, cozying it and stroking it, waiting and growing old and older and looking suddenly at the end of my life. Then the Huns broke — and I knew they were mine. They broke together to keep their formation, and I knew they were afraid of me and that I was going to kill them.

The Huns drove straight for the deck. A Focke-Wulf 190 is better on the deck than the kind of Thunderbolt I was flying then. I thought I could make up the advantage their machines gave them by this feeling I had in myself and by the fact that I was sure I had instilled in them that I was their master and was going to kill them.

I had had some experience in instilling this feeling into the Germans. Only a few days before the mere act of diving down to the deck with a Focke-Wulf, and of showing myself confident enough to be thrown to him as if I were a bone being tossed to a dog, had so panicked him, despite his mechanical advantage in a fight, that he had straightened out in a run from which he hadn't a prayer of a chance of emerging alive.

I was so intent on getting those Huns that I couldn't think of words to say into my radio to make sure my wing man was still with me. I wanted to make sure, but I couldn't take my eyes off those Huns for a second or I'd lose them, and besides I just couldn't think of any words to say into that radio. They wouldn't come out of my head and they wouldn't come into my mouth.

What happened to my wing man was that on the way down to the deck we were bounced by some other Jerries and he turned off into them to break up their attack. By the time he had done that we were as good as a million miles away from him — those two Huns, who were racing along the edge of their graves and myself, who was trying to push them in.

We were lost to the sight of anything in the air against the black, hunkered-up green of the forest of Compiegne. I didn't realize I was without any wing man to protect my tail until after I had got both Huns. One of them crashed in the open country at the edge of the woods and the second one went splintering into the middle of all those trees there.

Compiegne was where Hitler forced his armistice on the French, and it seemed to me a rather nice gesture to throw the bodies of two of his fliers down his throat there.

But in the meantime I was without any wing man. I found this out when, just after I pulled up away from the trees, tracers started shooting past me and I saw two more Focke-Wulfs on my tail, with nothing between me and them except the very thin, very naked air.

When you're down on the deck trading punches with a Focke-Wulf and spotting him that mechanical advantage, you have to have something to help you, even if it is only the feeling of fear in the enemy's mind. But these two new boys were not afraid of me. Oh, no! They came barreling right in, red hot for the kill. They hadn't even seen me shoot down those other two guys and quite likely they thought I was just some rabbit who had come down to the deck to get out of a fight going on upstairs. Psychology wasn't going to help me with them.

CHAPTER 7

So these two Focke-Wulf 190's came barreling in on me, red hot and sure of themselves and of a kill — so sure that they held their fire until they were right on top of me. The lead Hun was close enough to me when he started to fire for me to hear the ripped-out chugging of his machine guns and the soft poom-poom-poom of his cannon.

There was this sound, and at the same time tracers were going by me and my plane was starting to splinter around me. As I turned my head in a "what in the name of damnation is going on here" attitude, I saw a 20-millimeter shell go into my wing and saw the metal of the wing flower and open like a torn mouth and saw my tail quaking and shuddering with animal movements under the blows of more cannon shells. And I stared right into the millstream of bullets behind which sat the number one Hun looking like a doll there — looking inanimate and stolid and mechanical with his mask on.

I held my eyes into this millstream of bullets for what seemed a long time to me. I guess my eyes must have been pretty wide open, too. Then I threw my plane around and right into him, thinking, if I ram him I'll take the bastard with me and if I don't try it will be me going alone.

He had to pull up and over me. I stayed in a port turn because the Hun's wing man, number two, was still coming in. This number two guy ran out of guts and broke away. Right quick I threw my Thunderbolt into a starboard swing and let loose a burst at the guy, but didn't hit him. My nerves at the time were not conducive to accurate gunnery. I was starting to close on him and to give him another burst when I found out I had used up the last of my ammunition.

In the meantime the lead Hun who brushed over my head when I had swung in on him had pulled up and positioned himself for another attack. He made it while I still was in my starboard turn and just as I was discovering I had no more bullets left.

He had about a 30-degree deflection shot, but was giving it too much, and I could see his tracers hitting in front of my nose, maybe 30 or 40 feet in front. I kept watching his tracers walk toward me slowly as he corrected his aim, and it was one of the hardest things I had ever had to do. I had to keep along the line he was taking until the last minute. If I changed too soon he would anticipate it and I would lose my chance of surprising him off my tail. So I just kept still and watched the stream of tracers inch slowly, like a flooded river, lapping toward my cockpit and didn't think of anything, but just told myself in just these words: "Don, hold on to yourself; keep yourself steady and you'll get out of this all right. Don't panic, Don!" Like that, over and over again.

When the tracers got up to the edge of my cockpit I threw the airplane to port as hard as I could, giving it the maximum on the rudder and stick that you can without going into a spin. The whole plane shook — I could feel it shaking. That poor, old torn-out tail of mine was like a horse trembling, and I could feel the spine of the plane just bending. And I could feel that spine in my teeth, as if my gums were grinding under my teeth, but I held it there and held it and held it until I couldn't any more.

I was on the edge of a spin when I pulled out, and the tracers were still coming at me. I don't know who this Hun was, but he was a wise, old cookie all right — no kid at all, but a hard man who knew the tricks of the trade and knew he had a plane that could turn inside of mine and felt sure he was going to get me.

The best I could do with my turns was to keep him part-way off my tail and give him deflection shots at me, that is, keep my line of flight at an angle to his so that he would have to shoot ahead of me to try to hit me, which is the hardest kind of shooting to do.

I am not sure exactly how many times I sat still in the cockpit, just watching the tracers walk toward me and telling myself, "Don, hold on to your brains!" But I think it was three or four times.

Then, suddenly, in a turn, my plane flicked over on its back, and I was right over the trees of the forest of Compiegne. The whole fight had been from 50 to 100 feet above the trees. Now the trees reached up for me, and I had my head stuck down toward them, but I didn't panic. I just concentrated on remembering where that Hun was, and when I made my move to roll out of that flick I rolled in the direction where, if I came out at all, I would be alongside him and he would be off my tail at last.

It worked. I rolled out of my upside-down position, although I was that close to the trees that the whole air inside my cockpit seemed green with them. And when I came out right-side up again, there I was where I figured I would be — alongside the Hun and out of the angle of fire of his guns.

I found words for the radio transmitter then. "Help!" I screamed. "Help! I'm being clobbered!" I wasn't fooling. I really screamed. I heard some of the boys call down: "Where are you?" to me, but I couldn't take time to look and they never found me.

That Hun and I kept our eyes on each other. I had to wait for him to make an attack, and I think he suspected it. I think he knew I was out of "ammo" and that it was up to him to make the play.

A lot of things he did told me I wasn't bluffing him — not that crafty old cookie, not him. But when he turned to attack I turned in on him and charged him head-on. That gave him hardly any time at all to shoot. The best shooting range lasts less than 300 yards all told, and airplanes closing that distance at a combined speed of 700 miles an hour go those 300 yards in less than one second.

But this German wouldn't break off the attack before he had passed me. He was too smart and had too much guts for that. He knew he'd lose me if he did that. So the best I could do was to turn as he passed me and come alongside of him again. We did that for about fifteen minutes, reversing turns from head-on attacks. I couldn't outguess him and he couldn't outguess me.

We were at a stalemate in this duel of ours. For every thrust there was a parry, but I knew that all I had to do now was to stick with him until he ran out of ammunition, and that's what happened. He used up his last bullets and then he went home, and I climbed with a great surge into the sky, feeling I would like to find a cloud and get out and dance on it.

That fight was, perhaps, the most critical I have ever fought. I have had bigger triumphs, easier ones, but this one taxed every last bit of me. It showed me what I had learned and it taught me what I was. After it I felt there was no German alive anywhere who could keep me from killing him when I had an even break in the fight; or if the breaks went against me and he got them all, I felt I could keep him from killing me.

I had felt this way several times before, but now for the first time I knew the reasons. It was a handy feeling to have, for about a month after that the picture changed for the American fighter planes. They were taken off the defensive and put on the offensive and told to go out and clobber down every German that showed his face.

CHAPTER 8

When the bell rang for the big fight against Hitler's Luftwaffe last February, our twenty-six-year-old Colonel Donald Blakeslee, another Ohio boy, led into action as fine a team as I think any nation has ever been able to gather together.

The boys had a lot of natural ability; most of them had been so eager to fly that they had joined the R.A.F. or the R.C.A.F. before we had got into the war. Now their ability was tempered with experience. Their enthusiasm for the fight was sweeping and contagious. Each man was confident he would survive.

There is a pretty good test of the confidence of a group by the amount of money the individuals in it save. It isn't an infallible test, because there are a surprising number of people who just aren't interested in the future, even when they are sure they are going to live to see it. But Colonel Don Blakeslee's group stands high in allotments sent home. As a measure of my own confidence, I have been living on an average of about a dollar and a half a month since I got over to England and have been banking the rest to carry me through the lean, job-hunting days I expect after the war.

We started the offensive battles with 106 German aircraft destroyed to our credit, and by March 17 the group score had mounted to 200. By the second week in April we had 434 to our credit and were top scorers for the whole European Theatre of Operations. In the month from March 17 to April 16, we got more than twice as many German airplanes as we had in the two years of 1942 and 1943. Yes, there's no doubt that attack is the way to kill Germans. In my own case I shot down fifteen Germans from March 3 to April 1.

The whole attack has been a lifetime for many of our boys, and has been a long life for me. I started the battle by picking the best man I could get to fly on my wing — Johnny Godfrey, of Woonsocket, R. I., who doesn't like Germans. They killed his brother, Reggie, at sea, and the name Johnny has painted on his plane is "Reggie's Reply." He means it, too. The point about him is that he not only is a fierce, brave boy, but he knows his business as well.

To show how a team works even when a big brawl has boiled the team down to two men flying wing on each other, Johnny and I spent twenty minutes over Berlin on March 8 and came out of there with six planes destroyed to our credit. I got a straggler, and Johnny got one, and then I got another one fast. A Hun tried to outturn me, and this was a mistake on his part. Not only can a Messerschmitt 109 not outturn a Mustang in the upstairs air, but even if he had succeeded, there was Johnny back from his kill and sitting on my tail waiting to shoot him down. He was waiting, too, to knock down anybody who tried to bounce me off my kill.

There were Huns all around. Berlin's air was cloudy with them. The gyrations this dying Hun was making forced me to violent action, but Johnny rode right along like a blocking back who could run with the best. After two Huns had blown up and another had bailed out, Johnny and I formed up tight and went against a team of two Messerschmitts. "I'll take the port one and you take the starboard one," I told Johnny, and we came in line abreast and in a two-second burst finished off both of them. They were dead before they knew we were there.

Then a Messerschmitt bounced Johnny. Johnny turned into him and I swung around to run interference for him. The Hun made a tight swing to get on Johnny's tail, saw me and rolled right under me before I could get a shot in. I rolled with him and fastened to his tail, but by that time we were very close to flak coming up from the city. The Hun wasn't so worried about the flak. I was his immediate and more desperate woe, but flak wasn't my idea of cake to eat, and I didn't dare go slow in it while the Hun took a chance and put his flaps down to slow to a crawl.

Then I got strikes on him. Glycol started coming out of him, and I had to pass him. But Johnny had fallen into formation right on my wing and he took up the shooting where I had left off. He put more bullets into the Hun while I was swinging up and around to run interference for him. Then he said his ammunition had run out and I said, "Okay, I'll finish him," and I followed the Nazi down into the streets clobbering him until he pulled up and bailed out.

Teamwork is the answer to any man's score, but in the meantime there was plenty of competition within the team. Once a battle started there were a great many of the boys who saw in it what I saw — the chance to make a record that would come in handy later in life.

One of the best of them was Captain B. We were entirely unlike as people and came from different backgrounds as well as different parts of the country. But the odd thing is that he had the same idea as I and he had the same drive. He had had to quit on the eve of going to college, as I had, and for the same reason, and had joined the R.A.F. for the same reason as I, because he felt flying would give him the best chance to survive the war and to make a record in it that would provide him a leg up on a peacetime career.

Our scores mounted side by side. We flew every mission. One day he'd be ahead of me and the next day I would be ahead of him, and the first question each of us asked when landing was how much had the other fellow got.

Ground-crew men who could not understand the confidence each of us had in himself and who understood only the dangers of our work were a little puzzled by our attitude, I imagine. I remember one day early this month when I went up, under orders, to London to make a radio broadcast. I was a little sore about it until I saw it was raining and I said what was in my mind. "Well, I guess I won't miss anything today," I said, and the faces of the ground-crew men around me looked bewildered for a moment, and then they started to laugh. But it was just that while they understood the dangers they did not understand a man feeling completely able to handle those dangers.

On Thursday, April 6, Captain B. had twenty-one German planes destroyed to his credit and I had twenty-two. We went out to strafe some airports, and this is the kind of work all of us like the least. It is the most dangerous. A man can't rely on himself to carry him through. When he commits himself to an attack against a ground target protected by flak, he just throws his plane at it and the rest is luck. But this is necessary work — if the Germans won't fight in their planes in the air they have to be fought on the ground.

Captain B. had bad luck at one airport, while I was having good luck at another. He destroyed two Nazi ships and then I heard him over the radio saying flak had started glycol leaking out of him and he was gaining altitude. He said nothing after that for quite a while.

Although he was only twenty-two years old, he was a man of great composure and he believed in radio discipline. After that long silence he said in that soft, quiet, quick voice of his, "I am bailing out." And that was all he said — no goodbyes, no sorrys; nothing, just radio discipline.

That was the day my score ran up to twenty-seven destroyed. I didn't realize it until I put in my claim for five on the ground that I had seen burn, and Lieut. Grover C. Hall, Jr. (of Montgomery, Ala.) said, "Well, Don, that makes you the man who has destroyed more German planes than any American in two wars."

I asked him if he knew Captain B. had gone down, and he hurried off at once to B.'s squadron. Mess was very quiet that night. Captain B.'s squadron had scheduled a party, and they went through with it, but nobody's heart was in it and the girls who had come a long way to dance must have thought the Americans were just lumps.

A man likes to have a good score, but our training teaches us how important teamwork is, and the fellow who values his private score over his team either learns better fast or goes down.

I remember, on April 13, after I had run my score of destroyed to thirty, with twenty-three in the air and seven on the ground, we were over Schweinfurt. There were three Messerschmitts just sitting up there in front of me and not noticing me — just presenting themselves as the easiest shots I have had in this war so far. I was positive I was going to get all three.

Then I saw a Hun clobbering a Mustang mate of mine. I dropped my easy kills and dove on the Hun to bounce him off that Mustang. I didn't think about it at all; it was just a reflex action — nor do I regret having such reflexes. If the feeling for team action had not been developed as a reflex in me — something I and all the others boys can do without thinking — then I would have been dead or a prisoner of war a long time ago.

68182076R00028

Made in the USA
Middletown, DE
28 March 2018